The Beginner's Guide
to Abundance

The Beginner's Guide to Abundance

Activities for Learning the Law of Attraction and Creating the Life of Your Dreams

MELODY LARSON

To order additional copies of this book, contact:
Xlibris Corporation
1-888-795-4274
www.Xlibris.com
Orders@Xlibris.com
38696

Contents

Dedication

For mom, because it's never too late to reinvent your life.

For dad, who has always believed in doing so.

For Thomas, whose love and support helped me to do it.

And for Per, because I'm your proof it can be done.

You see things as they are
and you say "Why?"
But I dream things that never were,
and I say "Why not?"

– George Bernard Shaw

Author's note

*I*T WAS DURING *the final edits of this book that I came across a little paperback on my shelf that I hadn't read in 20 years. The book seemed to be jumping up and down like an excited child, pleading, "Read me! Read me!" Picking it up, I read the author's foreword and this is the message that I found there:*

"But then again, the things that this one told me! That we magnetize into our lives whatever we hold in our thought, for instance—if that is true, then somehow I have brought myself to this moment for a reason, and so have you. Perhaps it is no coincidence that you're holding this book; perhaps there's something about these adventures that you came here to remember . . . ."

– Richard Bach, *Illusions*

"We magnetize into our lives whatever we hold in our thought." That I had received this message 20 years ago nearly sent me off my chair. For here I am now, teaching others about this secret to success and happiness: By understanding and applying what is known as the Law of Attraction, we can deliberately create our reality.

I was provided a message as to my life purpose 20 years ago, but I wasn't ready to hear it. I was not ready then, but I am now. This book is the result of my professional and personal journey to figure out a methodology for mastering the Law of Attraction.

The universe is always sending messages and dropping clues in order to get you on your particular path of destiny. Know that you have brought yourself to this moment for a reason, just as I have. I am more grateful than you can imagine to be sharing this journey with you.

– Melody Larson

Welcome to the Law of Attraction

Do you find your present surroundings discouraging? Do you feel that if you were in another's place, success would come easier? It wouldn't, you know. Your real environment is within you. You make your own inner world, and through it, your outer world.

– Dr. Robert Anthony

Your life isn't happening 'without' you, willy nilly. You are in the driver's seat. Every day you are setting into motion a process that creates reactions. And within that process, you have the power of the universe to help you build the life you want to have.

– Oprah Winfrey

YOU ARE ABOUT TO CHANGE YOUR LIFE. There are no coincidences, no accidents. You have reached this page and are reading this, right now, for a reason.

The fact that you are reading this page tells me you are a person who is already on the way to creating a more meaningful and more fulfilling life. For you attracted this book to you through your thoughts, whether you are consciously aware that you did so or not. Congratulations!

You are about to learn what many of the wealthiest, most influential, most successful, most fulfilled, and most spiritually-centered people in this world already know: how to attract everything into your life deliberately, rather than by default. You need only understand one important law, and that is the Law of Attraction.

You see, the Law of Attraction states that like attracts like. If you are thinking prosperous thoughts, you will attract prosperity into your life. If you are thinking about suffering, you will attract suffering. If you are focused on the past, you will continue to relive that past instead of getting on with your life. Easy brings easy and hard brings hard. Success brings success and lack brings lack. Loneliness brings loneliness and love brings love.

Another way to look at the Law of Attraction is to say that it is all about cause and effect. For every thought (cause) there is a corresponding reality in your life (effect). In other words, and it is really important for you to get this, THOUGHTS BECOME RESULTS! Literally, your thoughts shape what shows up in your life. Your thoughts are what create your reality.

Because this is a law, it is completely impersonal. Thoughts create things, period. Whether the thought is "good" or "bad" makes no difference. Whatever you think about, you bring about. 100% of the time. It's that simple. And it's that powerful. Every single thing in existence is the result of this law! Pretty big stuff, indeed.

Now I can almost hear you saying, "But I think about what I want all the time and I never get it!" You may be thinking about it, but your focus is on NOT having it rather than on having it, and that is exactly what you get: not having it. It is not the object of your desire, but the focus of your attention, that is the cause that brings about the effect. What you intend is what's around the bend!

Let me give you an example. We often hear single people say, "I really want to be in a relationship but I just can't find the right person!" The problem here is, they are focused on that big BUT: the fact that they can't find the right person. Like attracts like. What you think about you bring about. And so what happens to these people? You guessed it! They never find the right person.

Imagine if these people would instead say, "I really want to be in a relationship and I intend to find the right person in the next 2 months!" What a different focus! And what happens? Bingo! Within 2 months the right person appears, because what you think about you bring about.

What you intend is what is around the bend! This is why so many of us consistently bring on more of the same in our lives. It's the notion of the self-fulfilling prophecy. If you expect things to be bad, they will *be* bad. But if you expect them to be good, they will *be* good.

Those who expect wealth, love, and fulfillment continually achieve more and more of those things in their lives, effortlessly. Those who expect debt, loneliness, and frustration get more and more of those things, and seem to continue to fight and struggle for what they want.

This is such exciting news! Now I know you may not be thinking that, but can you stay with me here for just a moment? Do you know why this is the best news you could ever hear? *Each and every one of us, you included, have the power to create ANY thought we want, to focus on whatever we choose. And that means that we can create any reality we choose!*

How? By being aware of how the Law of Attraction works!

Let me share a short analogy that will show you how the Law of Attraction works. After that, we'll take a look at the steps involved in detail.

I want you to imagine that you are holding a garden hose. You are standing next to a faucet, and you reach down and turn the handle on that faucet to full blast. Immediately, as you turn the handle, water begins to flow out of the faucet and into your hose. Even though you can't see it, water is flowing the *instant* you turn on the faucet. No argument there, right?

Okay. Now there is also just a moment or two that you have to wait before any water comes out the end of the hose. True? We know that the hose has some length to it and the water must travel through the hose before it can come out the end. But then, a few moments later, you see the evidence of this water when it splashes out onto the ground and muddies your sneakers.

Tell me, did you fret and worry in the few seconds that you were waiting for the water to come? Of course not! You knew that it WOULD come. You didn't doubt whether the water was available, or think about the mechanics of how the water would get to you, or question who put the water there in the first place, or worry that you were unworthy of this water flowing into your hose. That would be ridiculous!

The Law of Attraction works just like this garden hose. You ask for something that you want by turning on the faucet of your desire. You know beyond a doubt that the universe is answering your request the instant you turn on that faucet because when you ask, you always get a corresponding answer – cause and effect, remember?

You need only wait a bit for your thought to come down through the proverbial hose and manifest into your life in physical form. As long as you keep the faucet on and keep a hold of the hose, without kinking it up by doubting in any way that what you asked for is coming, wha-la! Out it does come indeed. That is the Law of Attraction in action.

Yet what do we do every day? We desire something to come into our lives, but then we get all caught up in doubt and worry. We get stuck on the logistics of how it will happen; or even worse, we tell ourselves we aren't deserving of what we want. We kink up the hose and then turn around and blame the hose for not working properly!

To receive the full benefits of the Law of Attraction, we have to stop blocking the flow of abundance that is always there for us. We can do this by becoming aware of exactly how this law operates.

The Law of Attraction is really a process that includes 5 steps:

1. Asking for what you want
2. Knowing that you are worthy of having it
3. Removing all doubt that it is coming
4. Remaining in a positive emotional state
5. Receiving it through right action

STEP 1: ASKING

In order to start this process with step 1, you have to know what it is that you truly want to have. You must figure out who you truly desire to be. You must decide what it is you wish to do with this precious life of yours. All options are now open to you. Every single possibility. The whole world is your catalog! If this idea overwhelms you rather than exhilarates you, then the activities in chapter 1 will help.

Many people start with a desire for material things, and that's just fine. It's important to have your worldly needs taken care of so that you are able to do what you love and live as who you want to be. Know, however, that materialism on its own is meaningless and will not bring fulfillment without some internal grounding.

So I suggest that you focus your desires not only on money and possessions, but also on relationships, health, and personal fulfillment. When you know who you truly are, when you do what you truly love to do, when you are in balance – then all the material things will line up effortlessly. Moreover, your life will be abundant in every sense of the word, not just materially speaking.

Once you are clear on your desires, be they material, emotional, physical or spiritual in nature, you must then focus on those desires on a consistent basis. While doing so, you must avoid sending the universe mixed messages by being sure you aren't focusing on what you DON'T want. You have to only focus on what you DO want.

For example, don't focus on getting out of debt, focus instead on being financially well off. If you try thinking of getting out of debt, you just end up worrying about the debt and, that's right, you attract even more debt! But if you think about all the wonderful ways your life will be enhanced as a financially well-off person, you will attract more money.

You can literally shape your reality just by focusing on what you want, bringing your desires into physical form; but, you must first clear out those mischievous little emotional bandits whose sole existence is to rob you of your efforts. You do this by moving through steps 2 and 3.

STEP 2: BEING WORTHY OF IT

So now you are clear on WHAT you want. The next step is to know on a deep and true level that you are worthy of your desires, every single one of them. You are more than your personality. You are an infinite being playing at being human in this lifetime! Those bandits in your head that tell you otherwise are a product of your ego, and it's time to give them the boot.

Your past belongs only to your personality and so has nothing to do with who you really are. Moreover, your current conditions are only a manifestation of who you *were* as a person before now. *You can literally wipe the slate clean at this very moment, for who you are from this moment forward determines who you will be and what will be in your future.*

I know this can be a hard concept to grasp, especially for people who have built up a lot of false beliefs about their so-called limitations. Likewise, people who hold resentments towards others for their accomplishments, possessions, or natural qualities have a hard time recognizing that they are just as worthy of those things. They are stuck in the-grass-is-always-greener game. I'm here to tell you: abundance is boundless and borderless.

Have vs. Have Not is a totally false and extremely limiting belief system. There is only Have and Have. You need only realize that you are worthy of having. If you are someone who thinks they don't deserve all that they desire, that the past equals the future, or that the grass is always greener on the other side, then you'll benefit hugely from the activities in chapter 2.

STEP 3: ERASING DOUBT

Next, in step 3, you have to remove feelings of doubt. You have to know with full conviction that all you desire will indeed manifest in your life. You have to expect it. We've been given a wonderful tool to make this process easy: our imagination. As children, we understood how to use our imagination. How sad that as adults we dismiss it as child's play. Imagination is the key to everything!

By consistently imagining yourself being, doing, and having all you desire as if it is already true, it becomes true in your mind. The universe gets your message and responds by saying, "Oh, there's a disconnect here between this person's vision and their reality. I better get to work ASAP on matching those two things up!" And so, it sets about bringing those desires to you in actuality.

Aha! Did you know that this is the whole reason we have imagination? We are equipped with imagination so that we may manifest our desires, just as sure as we are equipped with lungs so that we may breathe.

To use your imagination as it was originally intended, you repeatedly focus your attention on a specific vision in order to achieve specific results. Think about Olympic athletes who visualize their performance over and over before they actually do it. The universe needs specifics! If you say, "I want a new car." That's not enough. What make and model? What color? What features? It is the detail involved that separates imagining from mere daydreaming.

Thoughts literally shape the physical world. Cause and effect are everything. This is how the Law of Attraction works. If you don't believe me, check out what's happening these days in quantum physics. The so-called new science is proving it to be true. Step 3 is so absolutely critical, so let me give you an example:

Let's say you want to lose weight. If you keep getting on the scale every day and focusing on the unhappy number you don't want to see, if you keep grabbing at your flab and obsessing about it, if you keep staring at your current self in the mirror, full of self-loathing and disgust and hopelessness, then you are focusing on that as your reality. And so, that is exactly the reality that you continue to experience: more of the same, more overweight.

But if you instead taped a new smaller number on the scale and looked at it instead whenever you got on the scale, if you put a picture of your head on the body you'd prefer to have and looked at it instead of looking in the mirror, if you spent 10 minutes every day visualizing yourself being and feeling slimmer and acting like a healthy person acts, getting yourself all revved up on positive emotions, then that is what you would get instead.

Your thoughts would literally begin to change your body, your habits would improve effortlessly, and you would start to lose weight and eventually achieve a match-up to your visions. It won't happen overnight, but it will happen. It's a 100% guarantee! Just as it's a 100% guarantee that as long as you focus on your fat, you will stay fat.

I've hinted that another key part of step 3 is staying emotionally connected with what you desire. While you are mentally visualizing a desire as if it is already true for you, you must also get into feeling what it's like to have that desire. This is essential! When you have positive feelings you send out a high energy vibration to the universe, like one of those giant spotlights that department stores shine into the sky to attract customers to a special event. The universe will respond faster to your emotions than to just thoughts alone.

A final word on step 3: Your job is to focus only on WHAT you want and WHY you want it. That is all you have to do. It is the universe's job to figure out the WHO, WHEN, WHERE, and HOW. It always knows the fastest, easiest, and most appropriate way! It is in the details beyond the WHAT and WHY they we get stuck, get doubtful, and therefore get nothing! So do your job. Figure out what you want and why you want it, then relax and let the universe do its job.

I have found that step 3 is often the most difficult for many. We start off all fired up and excited, but over time we lose our momentum and ability to keep those visions and emotions sustained. When this happens, we slip back into step 2 again as we wrestle with our doubts, feelings of unworthiness, and lack of hope. That is why I have included so many activities in chapter 3 that are centered on this crucial step.

STEP 4: FEELING GOOD

Now we come to step 4. Like step 3, step 4 is about emotions, particularly the emotion of gratitude. The universe is expansive, abundant, and joyful! It doesn't understand or respond to lack and negativity. It is amazing how often we focus on the things we don't have while taking for granted all that we DO have. If you are a glass-half-empty person, the activities in chapter 4 will be extremely beneficial to you.

You must remain in a state of joy and gratitude. It's so important to feel good! Like attracts like. By having feelings that are joyful and grateful, you will attract even more things to be joyful and grateful about. You must be grateful not only for what you have in your life already, but for all that you "have" in your visualized life as well. Because it is yours already. You are only waiting for it to manifest into physical form. Remember the garden hose: positive thoughts and emotions keep the hose unkinked.

The universe LOVES to be thanked! It will respond to your appreciation with greater and greater abundance. All you desire will come faster than you could ever imagine.

STEP 5: ACTION!

Finally, step 5! Step 5 is about action. You can't just sit and wait for all you desire to magically appear. Visualization is like a magnet pulling your desires closer to you, but if you don't reach out and grab the stuff, the stuff will pass you by. Some things might literally land in your lap without any more effort than visualization, but to get most things it'll require some action on your part.

Note that by action I don't mean effort. It's more about understanding that what you desire may manifest in unexpected ways. You need to be open to, and act on, opportunities that show up. Remember that the HOW is not up to you to decide. Action, quite often, will be about not dismissing an intuitive nudge when you get one. When you have one of those little flashbulbs of brilliance go off, don't dismiss it! Don't tell yourself it's a ridiculous idea. Act on it without delay! Make it real before your emotional bandits destroy it. If I had let my bandits talk me out of writing this book, you wouldn't be benefiting from it right now.

You have to learn to recognize when an opportunity that will lead you to your desire is present in your life. The universe speaks in whispers rather than in trumpet blasts. You have to develop your intuition and pay attention to the clues the universe is leaving for you.

The last chapter in this book has activities designed to help you improve your intuition. Don't underestimate the power of developing it. Your intuition is how your higher self delivers the universe's messages to you. Without it, you may miss the opportunity to transform your visualizations into reality!

It was my intention that this little 'mini-lesson' give you a clearer understanding of what the Law of Attraction is, and how it works. Even if you are still a little unclear, the law will work for you anyway – it already does, remember? 100% of the time, just like gravity. The difference is that now you are making yourself consciously aware of it.

So don't worry: just by doing the activities in this book, you will move through the 5 steps naturally, and you will successfully apply the Law of Attraction pro-actively in your life, whether you fully understand how it works or not. Now, the only thing left for you to do is to try it out for yourself!

A word of warning, however: these activities are so uplifting and joyous that you may experience a natural high for life that you have hitherto never felt before! You are about to become a kid in the candy store of abundance. I also assure you of this: You absolutely cannot fail! No matter how many times you have tried to achieve your goals and have failed in the past, you simply cannot fail THIS TIME.

Whatever you have been or not been, achieved or not achieved, possessed or not possessed, is of no consequence whatsoever! You did not know about the Law of Attraction then, but you know it now, and all you desire will be so.

How to use this book

THE CHAPTERS THAT follow, chapters 1-5, correspond to the five steps just discussed in the introduction. In each chapter you will be given hands-on activities that take you through that particular step.

Although the chapters are in a sequential order designed to take you from step 1 to step 5, you do not have to start with chapter 1 and proceed chapter by chapter. You really can start anywhere you wish. For clarification and organization, the steps have been separated out, but in reality many of them are simultaneous processes, so do not be overly concerned with order.

You might start with the step that you feel most unclear on. For example, lets say you already know what you want (step 1) and you have no problem staying in a state of gratitude (step 4). However, what is tough for you is step 2 (knowing you're worthy of having it). You could start by going directly to the activities for step 2, located in chapter 2.

Or, you might start by choosing the activity that seems most enjoyable and exciting to you. Let's say you are going through the table of contents and the name of one of the activities jumps out at you and seems really interesting – go to that activity directly and start there. After all, it may be your intuition speaking to you!

In addition, I have created several activities that address the common life areas that people most often wish to improve: namely health, wealth, career, and relationships.

If you have a particular area that you are really eager to transform, you could choose to start with those activities directly.

Activities specifically designed for health:

> 7 – *Body talk*
> 18 – *Give your cells a pep talk!*
> 19 – *Healing waterfall*

Activities specifically designed for relationships:

> 21 – *A perfect match*

Activities specifically designed for career:

> 14 – *The business card*
> 20 – *Exciting career opportunity!*

Activities specifically designed for financial prosperity:

> 15 – *The money tree*
> 16 – *Checks in the mail*
> 17 – *All accounts positive*

Note that all the other activities in this book, in addition to these 9, will also allow you to work on these specific areas. They are designed in such a way that you can adapt them to whatever goals and dreams you have, including health, relationships, prosperity, and finding joyful work.

What I'm saying is that there is no right or wrong way to use this book! You can proceed chapter by chapter, or you can jump around a bit. You can work on only one activity at a time, or you can do several simultaneously.

Finally, please keep this in mind:

YOU DO NOT HAVE TO DO EVERY ACTIVITY IN THIS BOOK!

I have offered a wide variety of activities within each chapter, so that you can pick and choose, selecting the ones that really pop out at you. If an activity doesn't seem exciting or seems too difficult, by all means, choose a different one! You are to have fun and no activity should ever feel like a chore to you.

You will play best by following these five ground rules:

1. If it stops feeling fun, try another activity or take a break.
2. This is not a race. The whole way that the Law of Attraction works is through effortlessness.
3. Stay patient and never push yourself through an activity, or through this book, thinking that it will get you what you want faster. It won't! The moment you become impatient, you actually block the process.
4. It is always better to do an activity in writing than just in your head, so I suggest you purchase a journal or notebook for the occasion. There is also journal space included at the end of this book for those exercises that require pen and paper.
5. You actually have to DO the activities, not just read them, in order for them to work!

So relax and go with the flow. Enjoy focusing on all you want, knowing it will come at just the right time for you. Delve into these activities and experiences. Feel the magic, wonder, and bliss of unleashing your imagination, of flowing through each day in utter delight and gratitude, of knowing that all you desire is on its way!

Are you ready? Let's get started!

Chapter 1

If you don't know what you want . . .

Don't ask yourself what the world needs. Ask yourself what makes you come alive. Because what the world needs are people who have come alive.

– Harold Whitman

Activity 1

Getting out of Shouldville

On our journey to fulfillment we all must pass through the small town of Shouldville. Shouldville is the place where everybody does what they think they should be doing, according to the rules and expectations of their parents, their partners, their friends, their bosses, their coworkers, their church, their government, and/or their society. As boring and backwater a place as Shouldville is, many of us get stuck there instead of driving through.

In order to get out of Shouldville, you must get your thoughts beyond the radar screen of your current life. You have to give yourself permission to soar a little higher than you think you are allowed to or that you think you are currently capable of. Sometimes we are so focused on the mass illusion of what IS in our lives, that we can't figure out what we want because it ISN'T in our scope of vision.

To get back on the road again, try doing some idle fantasizing. (This is different than focused visualization, which you will do once you already know what you want.) Just let your mind drift with some thoughts of what could be instead of what is. You're not breaking any Shouldville laws, because this is just daydreaming, not action. No compliance cops are going to hunt you down and sentence you to a life of explaining to family, God and country why you thought you could do something nobody else was allowed to do.

Take out a pen as well as some paper. You can also use the journal space provided at the end of this book. While you can just do this in your head, it's better to write down your answers because we're going to return to them afterwards for a little follow-up activity.

Here's your assignment:

STEP 1

Complete the sentence, "It'd be amazing if . . . ." as many times as you can. See if you can come up with 20 statements for starters. You can always keep going, but don't give up after 5 or 7 or 12 – get at least 20!

For example:

It'd be amazing if I were offered a chance to travel across Africa by elephant.

It'd be amazing if I became a multi-millionaire from selling my talking socks invention.

It'd be amazing if I could quit my job and devote all my time to saving the Baloopa Bug from extinction.

Too wild for you? Okay. How about this one?

It'd be amazing if I could feel happy every single day.

STEP 2

Get writing! Go wild! Let yourself imagine all the things that you'd like to do, to be, to have. Nothing is off limits! More Money? More fulfilling work? Deeper relationships? Better health? A bigger house? Travel? Wealth?

Once you have exhausted your list, the next step is to go through them and rank them. Yes, every single one. If you could actually be, do, and/or have all these things, with the town of Shouldville in your rearview mirror, which one would be number 1 on your list in terms of its importance to you? Which one would be the least important, the last on your list? Which one would be number 2, number 3, and so on? Do this until you have put every one in order.

Now, look at your top 5. Do they excite you? Wouldn't it be amazing if all 5 of those things were happening in your life right now? Guess what: every single one of them is possible. Congratulations! You have just created a list of your top 5 intentions.

You now have a better sense of what you want. Don't worry if they seem vague or if they seem too huge and impossible right now. Remember, your job is the WHAT and the WHY only. Let the universe handle how all these things will unfold. Work with these top 5 as you proceed through this book, and you will begin to get a clearer picture of each one as you do so. You are about to cross the tracks and leave the town of Shouldville in your dust!

Activity 2

The recipe box

It is difficult to manifest your desires if you are not totally specific and clear in articulating what they are. This activity is designed for those who do better with a non-linear approach to figuring out what they want in life. Sometimes, just sitting down and making a wish list draws a blank. If you are one of those who cringe at the prospect of trying to put a list onto a blank page, you may do better with this activity.

You will spend some time making a "Recipes for Success" box. All the ingredients you need for a perfect life are in your mental creative kitchen. Much like a recipe box is divided into the categories of appetizers, soups and salads, entrées, desserts, and drinks, you can divide your life into categories of health, wealth, relationships, personal possessions, travel, spirituality, self-development, calling, or any other categories of your choosing.

You will need some supplies for this activity: a small box with section dividers, index cards, scissors, and glue or tape. You can buy a recipe box or photo box, which already comes with dividers and often with blank cards, or you can make your own from a shoebox or other box.

STEP 1

Once you have your box, decide on the life categories you would like to use, and write them on your section dividers. You can use the list above, or come up with your own. Now, place a bunch of blank recipe cards or index cards into the box. At this point, you will not worry about which recipe cards will go into which sections. That comes later.

STEP 2

Your next task is to gather your "recipes". While reading books or looking at magazines, collect or tear out words, quotes, poems, photos, or other images you find that please you, for whatever reason. Paste each one onto a recipe card or index card.

Continue to do this until you feel you have collected enough or until you begin to see a pattern emerging in the types of things that attract you. There is no rush, no hurry. So don't pressure yourself. Take as long as you need to peruse and pick out items. This should be a fun, natural, no-pressure activity! When you feel you have gathered enough cards, you are ready to move on to step three.

STEP 3

Step three is to sort your cards and place each of them into an appropriate life category. As you do this sorting process, you will begin to see a very clear picture of what your desires are for every area of your life.

One thing that may happen during step three is that some categories will have a lot of cards while others may have very few. Categories packed with recipes are clear indications that you have a strong desire to spice up that area of your life. Other categories may be sparse for a variety of reasons: you are less clear on what you want regarding that area of your life, you already have a lot of desires met there, or you have more mental "blocks" about that aspect of your life than other aspects.

You know you are blocked when you feel bad about that area of your life: perhaps you feel unworthy of achieving fulfillment, or the task of fulfillment seems too overwhelming to achieve. If so, still keep collecting for those other categories that are less full. This collection process will actually help you to get clearer and to feel better about your ability to succeed in that area.

Ponder your items once you have them sorted, not always taking them at face value. For example, let's say you have collected a lot of items that are related to wardrobe. You chose to put them in your 'wealth' category because you wish you had the money to buy these things. Let me ask you this: WHY do you want these particular clothing items? Do they reflect a totally different style than what you have now? Maybe it isn't more wealth, but a change in personality that you desire.

By reflecting further, let's say that you do indeed have a desire to present a different image of yourself. Say, one that is more sophisticated. Again, ask yourself WHY you wish to look or be more sophisticated. How would dressing this way make you feel? When you can answer that second why question, you are really onto your truest desires beyond money or the collection of stuff.

Use this box whenever you need inspiration or clarity. Refer to it when working on some of the other activities in this book. Or, if you wish to work on your intuition, take out your box and randomly draw a card. Know that the card you've selected is the perfect recipe needed at that time to serve up a tasty life dish.

Meditate on what the card signifies to you. I promise you will be given an answer if you question why you drew that particular card in that particular moment in time. You attracted it to you, after all.

Activity 3

Bliss list blitz

This activity serves several purposes:

- You can use it as a brainstorm for getting clearer on what you want, step 1 in the Law of Attraction process. That is its intention for this chapter. Once you've done so, keep this list handy, because it also works for steps 3 and 4.
- You can use this as an instant emotional pickup if you are feeling less than good. Just reading over this list will make you feel happy, and if you really take time to visualize and imagine each item on your list, you will feel totally fabulous!! I guarantee it.
- This list serves as a gratitude check, for you will discover that so many things you love and appreciate are already in your life. The universe loves gratitude and will provide even more things for you to feel grateful for.
- Just by making this list, you are signaling your desires and so the universe begins instantly working on getting any things to you that you don't already have.

So, you can see why I call this a Bliss Blitz!

Whip out a piece of paper and something to write with, or use the journal space in this book. Make a list of everything you love. I mean everything. Don't stop writing until you have at least 50 things, and shoot for 100! To get started, think about the 5 senses and then keep going from there.

What smells do you love? What sounds? What do you love to taste? What textures feel fabulous on your fingers? Write them down. Once you are rolling on those, think next of things you love, such as puppies, cars, ink pens, or Tuscan villas. Whatever things float your boat. Then move on to activities you like to do. How about favorite people, even those you've never met, but admire? How about favorite places to visit? You get the idea. Just keep writing!

Do you have at least 50? Good. Now go through your list and circle the things that you love but don't yet have in your life. Your circled items can become the basis for your WANT list as you proceed further in this book. Put a star or a check mark next to the things you love and already have in your life. Use those items for step 4: gratitude. Read this list whenever the desire strikes you, and add to it as more things come to mind!

Activity 4

Your perfect day

What would you do with your life if you could step out of your daily routine for an entire 24 hours? Money is no object. All the obligations you currently have, caring for your family, going to your job, everything – are completely removed. All options are open to you! Also, imagine you have been given a magic power that allows you to travel from place to place instantly, without having to worry about flights, trains, or time. Sound marvelously fun? It is!

This activity has 4 steps:

STEP 1

Read the instructions to get you fantasizing, and STOP reading further where it says to do so. The reason for this is that after you have created your perfect 24 hours, there will be some guidelines to help you interpret the significance of your daydream. If you look at them ahead of time, it may influence what you see in your mind's eye, and that will limit you.

STEP 2

Do the visualization.

STEP 3

Write down any notes you wish to make to help you remember your experience.

STEP 4

Complete the analysis using the guidelines provided.

Caveat: Do this activity only at a time when you won't be disturbed and when you are already in a fairly relaxed and good mood. If you are stressed, depressed, or otherwise upset, you will find it difficult to create any positive images, so this will just leave you frustrated and feeling even worse.

INSTRUCTIONS

Sit or lie down in a comfortable position. Be sure you won't get cold. Close your eyes and take 5 deep, long, slow breaths to get yourself good and relaxed. Aaaaah.

Now, you will spend a few moments just pondering all the possible things you might like to do during this 24 hour period. Do you want to travel? Meet someone famous? Try something you've never tried before? You are completely free to go anywhere, be with anyone, do anything your heart desires. Spend some time exploring the possibilities until you hit on something that feels exciting.

When you feel you have that strong sense of excitement, go with it. Imagine yourself doing that thing you desire to do and just flow with it and create a whole 24 hour experience for yourself, starting with that one thing. Just let yourself go. This one thing may take up the whole time, or you may just start there and then move on to other things. There are no rights or wrongs to this! Trust me, your imagination will take you just where it most wants to go.

Okay. STOP READING NOW. Begin your perfect day visualization!

Alright, did you have fun? Don't you feel wonderful right now? Take a few moments to make any notes of anything you wish to remember about this experience.

You are about to learn so much about your true desires. You'll need to go through and answer the questions below, either mentally or on paper. When you are finished, you will have gained insight into your true self that is so significant it may put you on a whole new life path.

When I did an activity similar to this, I discovered a deep and long-lost desire to write again, something I had dismissed as a "childhood fantasy" that I could never make a serious living at. Well, well, what do you know. Here you are reading my book. So don't underestimate the importance of letting your higher self have a voice in your life. It always knows what is best for you, every single time!

Let's begin to explore your visualization. The questions below offer possible interpretations, but only you can fully decode the meaning of your visions.

1. *Did you spend your day in your own home or somewhere else?*
   Spending your day at home is very significant. It may imply that you are overworked and need rest, or that you have a desire to work for yourself, or that you are weary of living up to external expectations and wish to be true to who you really are.
2. *Did you travel to faraway places you have never been before?*
   This is often a sign that you are longing to expand your horizons and are ready to take some risk in order to bust out of the life that is now too small for you.

3. *Did you spend your time pursuing a particular activity?*

    If it was an activity you have always wanted to try but you have never actually done so, now is the time! If it was an activity you are already doing, consider the possibility that this may be a life calling for you, that you may find your life purpose hidden in it somewhere.

4. *Were you alone, or did you encounter and interact with many people?*

    Again, if you were alone you may be needing some down time in your life – either to rest, or to be able to get your creativity flowing so you can do some dreaming and goal-setting. If you encountered many people, you may be on the hunt for others that can support you in achieving your new dreams.

5. *Did you spend time with one significant person? Was this person someone real or made up?*

    Either way, take time right now to describe this person in detail, from looks to personality to anything they did or said to you. I cannot overemphasize the importance of having one key person show up and share your day with you! This is someone you strongly desire to manifest into your real life! If this person is already in your real life, congratulations! If not, keep visualizing more experiences with this person and know that eventually, in some way, he or she will appear in your future.

6. *Summarize this adventure using 5 adjectives. If you had to describe it in only 5 words, what words would you choose?*

    Write them down. Now look closely at these adjectives. They are how *you* desire to be, or to feel – and it is crucial that you begin designing a life that allows you to be and feel this way on a daily basis!

    I encourage you to do this activity as many times as you desire. Each time, your visualization will become more and more clear and elaborate, giving you more and more insights into your true self's wants and needs, even as far as helping you to discover the reason that you are here on Earth and what your life purpose is.

Chapter 2

Because you're worth it!

We ask ourselves, "Who am I to be brilliant, gorgeous, talented and fabulous?" Actually, you are you NOT to be? You are a child of God. Your playing small doesn't serve the world.

– Marianne Williamson

Activity 5

The judgment jar

Are you one of those people who has an opinion about everything and everybody? Do you find yourself frequently complaining about things or criticizing others – or worse, criticizing yourself? Well you're not alone. It's a modern epidemic and it is killing dreams.

Whatever you focus on becomes your reality, whether you are focused on something good or on something bad. If you are constantly judgmental or critical about certain events or people or behaviors, the universe will just keep putting more of those things into your life, because by focusing on them you are asking for them.

The first step in ridding yourself of this destructive habit is to make yourself aware of when you are thinking judgmental, critical thoughts – about others or about yourself. To do this, you need a judgment jar. Get yourself a jar, any jar will do. Make a label for it that says Judgment Jar. Next you will need some scrap paper, probably a lot of it at first!

Now. Every time you find yourself thinking a thought that is judgmental, critical, or negative in any way, about someone else, something else, or about yourself, write that thought on a scrap of paper and deposit it into your jar. As you do so, say to yourself, "I remove this negative thought from my ego-driven mind. I now choose to think as a higher being. I observe rather than judge from this moment forward."

When your jar becomes full, take out all the thoughts and rid yourself of them. You can burn them, recycle them, bury them, or float them out to sea, but let them go! When you do so, say to yourself, "I am now free of judgment and criticism. I now know that variety is necessary in life. It is wonderful that each of us has so many options to choose from!"

I considered myself a fairly positive person until I tested out this exercise. My judgment jar was nearly full by the end of the first day! After one month, I reduced the number of items in my jar to just 4.

Activity 6

Prison break

Imagine someone sitting in a prison cell. Imagine they are serving a life sentence. Imagine that person is you.

What have you sentenced yourself to for life? Do you have doubts that your dreams are too big for you? Do you feel unworthy of all you desire? Do you suffer from jealousy, fear, disappointment, hopelessness? Do you find your work to be a total drudgery? Are you out of shape? Are you in debt? Do you make less money than you'd like? Are your relationships less than satisfying, or worse, are they non-existent? Would you like a second chance?

Look at your cell door. Take a good look at it. The key is hanging in the lock, and it has been hanging there the whole time. Listen. It's quiet, isn't it? There are no guards, nobody's there but you. Your prison sentence is self-imposed and your current life is an illusion of your own making. Break out of the prison you have made of your life. No matter what you did to "deserve" it, it is time to set yourself free!

The key that unlocks your prison door is imagination.

Take out 2 sheets of paper, or use the journal space provided. On the first sheet, make a list of all the things that you are unsatisfied with in your life. Be ruthless. Be a harsh grader! If there is anything in your life that is less than totally fulfilling, put it on your list. If anything you are, have, or do in your life leaves you feeling less than totally joyous, put it on your list. You will feel pretty lousy when you're done with this part, but hang in there.

Now, on the second sheet, cross reference your first list and write down what the opposite of every item on that list would look like. For some of the items, the opposite might be no longer doing them or having them in your life at all! That's just fine. When you have completed your second list, throw away the first sheet. You are now free. Your dues have been paid, and then some! Use the second sheet to begin setting your goals and building the dream life you deserve. Open that prison door and walk out into the light of a beautiful new beginning!

Activity 7

Body talk

This activity is designed to help you meet your goals surrounding better health. Whether you wish to have more energy, to lose weight, to have clearer skin, or to heal yourself of a serious or terminal illness, the principle is the same. You must rid yourself of any resentment, guilt, or feelings of unworthiness you have surrounding your body. Until you can do that, setting a health goal will never really work because your negative feelings, especially if you are not consciously aware of them, will block your success.

If you are feeling a strong desire to improve your life in the area of health, take a stab at this activity. It will help you to clear away any negativity so you can then get to the task of successfully using many of the visualization activities in this book to achieve your health dreams.

In this activity, you will write a letter to your body. Then, you will have your body write a letter back to you. Here are some guidelines to get you going.

A.   Letter to your body

> *Dear body,*
>
>> *I am so grateful to you for . . . .*
>> *What I most love about you is . . . because . . .*
>> *I love that you are able to . . . because . . .*
>> *I apologize to you for . . . .*
>> *What I will try to do for you from now on is . . .*
>> *What I would like you to do for me is . . .*
>>
>> *Thank you again for being so wonderful to me! I now know that you are the perfect body for me to have in this lifetime and that I, in fact, chose you as my partner for this lifetime.*
>> *And so, having realized this, I now know that we are a powerful, unstoppable, and highly effective team. From this moment on, we will work together and we will achieve absolute perfect health!*
>
> *Thankfully,*
> *(your name)*

B. Letter from your body

Dear (your name),

I am so grateful to you for . . . because . . .
I forgive you for . . .
What I love about you is . . . because . . .
What I would like you to do more for me is . . . .

In exchange, I will do all the things you have asked me to do for you, and I will get to work on those items immediately! Thank you for remembering our partnership. Please forgive yourself for forgetting. From now on, we will indeed work together and we will achieve absolute perfect health!

Faithfully,
Your body

Release the falsehood that your body and your mind are separate. Know that your thoughts are responsible for whatever state your body is in. By changing those thoughts and by replacing negative feelings with positive ones, you can take responsibility for recreating your physical state.

Activity 8

Pamper your senses

This is a deceptively simple activity, but it sends a signal to the universe that you have realized your self-worth. Worthiness is like a flashing light that blinks out into the darkness. When the universe sees your light, it knows that you are ready for your desires to manifest. It then gets busy bringing them to you!

Here's what you do:

Every day, you must do one thing that satisfies each of your senses: sight, smell, taste, touch, and sound. That's 5 things a day.

I suggest that you start by making a list for each of these senses.

- What do you love to look at?
- What smells send you into a fit of reverie?
- What tastes make you tingle?
- What do you love to feel against your skin?
- What sounds are music to your ears?

Take a look at your Bliss List Blitz activity from chapter 1 as another place to gather up ideas. Be sure each of your senses gets to experience one thing it loves every single day! Don't underestimate the importance of pampering yourself. It is not selfish or shallow to do so.

Activity 9

That's just like me!

Do you ever suffer from envy, jealousy, feelings of longing or low self-worth when you see somebody else having something you don't have? Well, welcome to being human! But I hope you realize by now that whatever someone else has, you can also have. You can be, do, or have anything. You only need to believe that you are deserving of it and capable of it.

If you resent others for what they have, you prevent yourself from ever having it. This is very important to understand, because all of your work with this book will be for naught if you don't wrap your mind around this: If you resent others for what they have, you prevent yourself from ever having it.

When we resent others for what they have, we are sending out a very strong message to the universe that we DON'T have it. We do this because our emotions are in the negative: we are consumed by longing and lack and what the universe hears is, "I don't deserve to have those things myself, so please don't ever send them my way."

This little activity is incredibly powerful for turning these emotions around. It will help you change your message to, "I see that person having those things, and I think it's really great! I think I'd also like some of that, please!"

Here's all you have to do:

Every time you find yourself envying someone else, say to yourself, "That's just like me! That's exactly who I am!" Your ego will hate this reaction and will try to convince you that you are lying, but keep at it.

Eventually, your feelings of envy will switch to feelings of empowerment and connection. When you stop envying, you'll know that you really GET that this is an abundant universe. You get that there is enough for everyone and so comparison, therefore, really becomes completely ridiculous. By doing this activity consistently, you change your message to the universe from a "No!" to a "Yes!"

Chapter 3

Keeping the focus

No one would send for a set of sheets and say, "Twin, Queen, whatever you've got," but the divine fulfillment service, interpreting our mental yearnings, gets countless requests as unclear as "I'd really like a job," and "It would be awfully nice to have a husband." It's no wonder so many people are living lives that don't fit.

– Victoria Moran

Activity 10

Intention statements

Intention statements are designed to focus you and get you clear on:

- what you want
- why you want it

Nothing will rev you up like a strongly crafted intention statement! When yours is polished and complete, you will have sent out a message to the universe that you mean business! The response will be, "Well okay then, I see you aren't messing around here, so I'll get on this for you ASAP!" And then, all sorts of things will begin to happen that allow you to fulfill your intention almost effortlessly.

Remember, it is your job to get very clear on WHAT you want and WHY you want it. It is the universe's job to handle the who, when, where, and how. There is no particular method for making an intention statement, as they are highly personal, but I'm including some guidelines and examples to get you started.

Ways to write your statement:

1. *I'm so joyous and fulfilled now that . . . . because I am now able to . . . . This feels . . . . !*
2. *I intend to . . . . in order to/that will . . . . and as a result . . . . Achieving this makes me feel . . . . !*
3. *I am now . . . . and this has allowed me to have . . . . As a result, I have easily and effortlessly achieved my desires to . . . . Because of this, I feel . . . !*

Here are 2 examples:

EXAMPLE 1

This is an intention statement that a client of mine, an instructor, created after I took him through this exercise. He had received repeated student complaints and his boss had him on a plan of improvement. If he couldn't turn things around, he would lose his job.

He chose to use version number 3 from the previous page:

I am now a dynamic, interactive, and incredibly creative instructor that excels at teaching students how to teach themselves by getting off the stage and providing learning-centered activities. *This has allowed me*, and my students, *to have* meaningful and motivating classroom experiences every time. *As a result, I have easily and effortlessly achieved my desires to* move from being on a plan of improvement to being nominated instructor of the year*! Because of this, I feel* worthy, confident, useful, and grateful that I am able to help so many students improve not only their academics, but their lives.

He didn't receive instructor of the year that year, but he did receive it 2 years later! That's the power of intention.

EXAMPLE 2

Here is my own intention statement that I wrote when the idea for writing this book first came to me. Notice that it follows example 2 from above:

I intend to create a wildly successful book on 30 simple and fun activities *that will* teach hundreds of thousands of people how to become co-creators of their own lives! *As a result* of this book, I will have taken another major step towards fulfilling my life purpose of teaching others to know themSelves. *Achieving this* dream of being a wildly successful author that helps others realize and unleash their full spiritual potential *makes me feel* purposeful, significant, humble, grateful, amazed, actualized, and absolutely blissful!

Okay, now it's time to write an intention statement of your own! At first, just write. You can then go back and tweak it to your liking. Keep rewording it until it emotionally charges you up. When you hit a state of reverie and bliss, you know you have it just right.

You can write more than one intention statement if you desire, but I would keep it to a maximum of 4, say one for each key area of your life: health, wealth, relationships, and career/purpose. You should read your intention statement(s) every single day, several times a day if possible. Doing so helps keep you focused on and connected to what you desire to manifest. Once it's written, however, you can also relax, knowing that just by writing it, you have set the wheels of attraction into motion!

Activity 11

What/Why wheels

If you found activity 10 on intention statements too verbal for your taste, the What/Why wheel is a more visual way to make an intention statement. You can also use the wheel as a brainstorming activity to gain clarity before you write an intention statement.

In the center of the wheel, write down what it is you wish to be, have, or do. In other words, what is your desire or goal? Then, around the wheel, put all the reasons why you wish to achieve that goal. Make a spoke in the wheel for each why. You may have only 4 spokes, like in the picture below, or you may have 6, or 9, or even 20 spokes!

It looks something like this:

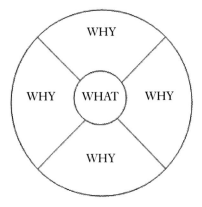

Make a wheel for each desire or goal that you have. I suggest starting with 4 wheels: one for career, one for health, one for relationships, and one for wealth. That way, you get a balanced, workable wagon that will get your life rolling. A 3-wheeled wagon isn't going to roll. You must always think about balance, so focus on all the major areas of your life at the same time. Don't worry; the universe can effortlessly handle 4 goals. It could handle 1000 goals! But 4 is what I would suggest you try for now. If you don't have 4, try 2. A bicycle functions just as well as a wagon.

Activity 12

Dream boards

Dream boards are like art pieces of attraction. They are collages of visual images that represent all of your dreams, intentions, and goals. There is nothing more powerful or more wonderful feeling than spending time each day looking at your own personal dream board. It'll get you jumping like a puppy in a playfield as you look at all those things that are about to come true for you in your life!

Dream boards are one of the best ways I know for helping you stay focused and connected to your desires. There is no right or wrong way to make a dream board. The easiest way to make one is by tearing or cutting out photos from magazines that best represent what it is you want to have in your life and pasting them on to a large piece of paper, collage style.

You might include your dream car, house, photos of places you'd like to visit or live in, or pictures of people you'd like to know. You can also search the net for specific products and then print them out for using on your board. I loved the activity of going to a car dealer online and custom "ordering" my car and then printing it out and putting it on my board!

For some items, it can be difficult to find a photo. Say you want to be able to visualize your dream job but can't find a photo. In this case, you could use the business card activity from this chapter and put that card on your dream board. Or, you could write the amount of salary you wish to have and how you desire to earn that money and put that on the board. So you don't always have to use just photos.

Get creative! Even if you don't have artistic talent, you can draw what you desire. I have also put words or phrases on my dream board regarding how I wish to be. Anything goes, as long as it gets you going!

Tips:

- it needs to be large enough for you to really see each image on the board clearly
- use any material, from poster board to a remnant from a cardboard box
- frame it for real WOW! impact and hang it as art in your bedroom, office, or other semi-private area of your home
- make 1 big board that tells a story: put your house on the board, and next to it your car, and off to the side your job, and in another area your weekend activities, etc. In this way, you create a visual routine for your perfect new life

- make a separate board for each life area: career, relationships (friends, family, romance, mentors, etc) health, and wealth (money as well as what you want to buy or do with it)
- make a mini "travel size" board that you can keep in your purse or briefcase and look at it frequently throughout the day!

Activity 13

Grant letters

This is a great activity to keep yourself in alignment with your desires once you've decided what it is you'd like to have. You can also use just the first part of this activity as a way to brainstorm what your desires might be.

STEP 1

First, you will write a letter addressed to the universe. You can address this letter to whomever you would like, such as your Universal Granting Committee, your Subconscious, God, your Higher Self, the Department of Creative Intelligence . . . whatever feels powerful and fun for you.

In this letter you will list your specific desires and ask that they be granted. For each desire, only describe WHAT you want and WHY you want it. You know that the universe will take care of the how, who, where, etc. and that is why you are writing. I suggest that you include at least one desire for each area of your life, such as wealth, health, relationships, self development, career, or other area that is of importance to you.

Here's a sample letter:

Dear Universal Management Team,

I'm writing to you because I have recently realized that I am a powerful co-creator of my own life and am now ready to do some co-creating with you. I know it is my responsibility to decide what I want and why I want it, and that it is your responsibility to fulfill each desire I have by taking care of the how, who, what, where, and when.

So, I have thought about my wants in great detail and am now ready to request their fulfillment from you. The desires I have that are vitality important to me right now, that I have a very passionate desire to fulfill, are below. I am sure I will have more in the future, but for now, I ask that you grant the desires listed and immediately go about the task of making them happen:

1. *It is my powerful and passionate desire to fulfill my natural abundant state of being a total money magnet. And so, I intend to achieve an annual income of $125,000 within 1 year's time, as of (date). I intend this because I wish to feel the security and relief of knowing that money is plentiful enough for me to maintain the lifestyle I desire, so that I may instead use my energy to focus on my life purpose.*

2.   *I have a powerful and passionate desire to return my body to the perfect form it was meant to be, and so I intend to weigh 125 pounds two months from now, by (date). I intend this because I wish to feel the thrill of buying clothes that make me feel fabulous, and because I want to feel the utter power of knowing I am in the best shape I can be in to live a long and prosperous life!*

I am utterly confident in your divine creative abilities to make these desires a reality in my life, and I am so grateful to you for your partnership in co-creating with me!

I promise to do my part in this co-creative process, which is to stay focused on the what and the why of each of my desires by imagining them as if they are already true on a daily basis. Please let me know if there is anything I can do further, and I will remain open to any signs.

Sincerely and gratefully,
Name

STEP 2

Next, you will draft a response letter from the universe, ideally typed, and then mail the letter to your home address. In a few days, when you receive the letter, it will serve to reinforce not only your desires but your belief and trust in the process.

I recommend reading this response letter to yourself often as a way of keeping up your momentum and positive feelings about your desires coming true. You may even choose to write and send yourself follow up letters, if you find this process is one that really clicks for you.

Here's the sample return letter:

Dear Name,

We are delighted that you have chosen to consciously take part in the co-creative process, and that you have asked for your desires to be fulfilled! And of course, we wish to inform you that every one of your requests, as outlined specifically below, have been granted in full by our team.

Our team members are already in action and are working round the clock to manifest your desires! We only ask that you remember to fulfill your part of the co-creative process, which is actually profoundly enjoyable, and that is to simply stay focused on your desires and to feel what it would be like for you to have them manifest. Keep visualizing and staying passionate about your desires! That is all you must do.

Please maintain a copy of this letter as proof of our guarantee that all you have asked for is now yours. It is our humble suggestion that you read this letter often and dwell frequently on the wonders therein that are about to manifest in your life!

Items granted to Name, residing at (address):

- *An annual income of $125,000 is now yours. You will receive this income no later than (date you specified), if not before.*
- *You will weigh exactly 125 pounds on the date of (insert date), if not before.*

Congratulations!
With Utmost Pleasure and Delight,
Your Universal Management Team

Activity 14

The business card

This is an excellent and simple activity for manifesting your ideal job, career, or calling. Create a business card that includes your intended business name, job title, website address, etc. and put it in places where you can focus upon it daily. As you focus upon it, visualize what it would be like for you to be DOING what it says on the card, including how it would feel.

There are many software programs that have business card templates you can use for free, including Microsoft Word and Microsoft Publisher. If you choose, you can even buy printer paper that allows you to print business cards that are pre-perforated. This isn't necessary, however. You can just as easily make a card, print it out on regular paper or card stock paper, and then cut it out. It is up to you how realistic this card needs to be, but it must make you FEEL excited when you look at it!

Make several cards and put them in places where you will see them often. I made my cards and kept one on my nightstand, taped one to my bathroom mirror, put one on my computer monitor, one on my fridge, and one in my wallet. You get the idea.

You now have a powerful tool to keep your mind and your heart fully focused on your business or career goal. Because you have made it become very real for you, and are focusing on that intention daily, it will become your reality! How? Not your problem, remember? Just stay focused on what job you want and why it would be so wonderful to have it.

Activity 15

The money tree

This activity assists you in developing your wealth consciousness. Each and every person on the planet is a money magnet, including you. If, through conditioning, you have not believed so, know now that it IS so.

One sure way for money to flow into your life is for you to get very good at spending money. "But I don't have any money to spend, otherwise I wouldn't be asking for money!" Now, calm down. I'm talking about spending in your imagination only. In your imagination, in the spiritual realm, you must spend, spend, spend! You must get creative and learn to be the big spender that you are!

It takes a little effort to put this activity together, but this is no ordinary craft project. Isn't it worth the time when the results will bring you total financial freedom? So, let's get started on this incredible wealth attraction activity.

First, photocopy 1 side of a twenty dollar bill 50 times. Ideally, copy in color. Note: do not copy double-sided or you will be illegally creating counterfeit money! I assure you that by copying in the way I've suggested, it is perfectly legal. You may also purchase play money for this purpose, which is available in many toy stores. If you make copies, cut out each "$20 bill."

Next, purchase a cardboard or Styrofoam cone from a craft store, or make one yourself. Using pins, glue, or tape, cover the cone with your $20 bills. Start at the top and layer the bills in rows until you have covered the entire cone with all 50 bills. You now have a money tree that totals $1000!

But here is the really fun part! At least twice a day, perhaps when you awaken and before you go to bed, spend some time gazing upon this tree and imagine yourself spending all of the money on it, every single dollar. Select something that you'd like to buy with the $1000. It may be one big item, or several items. You can even pay bills if you'd like.

The rules are:

1) You MUST spend the entire $1000 each time. Imagine yourself taking the $1000 from the tree and buying what you want. Because it is a tree, know that the money will always grow back! Know that the money will be there the next time you go to the tree to buy something again. By doing this activity

you are spending $2000 daily. If you do this every day for 1 year, you will spend $730,000!

2)   *You must really visualize yourself buying the items.* What will you do with them? How does it feel to have them? How does it feel to have this income coming in on a daily basis?

3)   DON'T put money in savings! More is coming the next day, and the next. So there is no need to hoard. Let it flow, signaling to the universe that you are abundant!

Alternatives:

- If you're feeling really open to attracting wealth, make a tree that has more than $1000 on it.
- In addition to mentally spending, use a checkbook ledger or other system to record all of the purchases you make. You can then review this list and imagine having all those items all over again, whenever you feel like it.
- Instead of twice a day, mentally spend the $1000 every time your eyes fall upon the tree.
- Instead of a tree, place the money on a lampshade and spend it every time you happen to turn on that lamp. And yes, pick a lamp that you turn on often!

Activity 16

Checks in the mail

Oh sweet abundance. How wonderful to get a check in the mail. Imagine getting a check in the mail every month for doing something you absolutely love to do! This activity places the message in your mind that you are already doing what you love and getting paid exactly what you desire for that work. Because you are asking and are living it in your mind, it is only a matter of time before it becomes a reality in your life.

This activity has 3 simple steps:

1. Decide what you want to do for a living.
2. Decide how much money you want to make each month doing it.
3. Write yourself a check each month from the person or company you want to work with or for, even if you wish to work for yourself.

You can mentally see the check arriving and imagine yourself depositing it, but to really make this fun, why not write yourself an actual check and mail it to yourself each month? Use a real check, or even design one on your computer with the company address and logo. You can get as creative as you need to make the check feel real to you, but it will be fine if you do this activity only in your mind as well.

Either way, expect abundance! Focus monthly on what it is like to get paid for what you love to do. Visualize the outcomes in your mind and they will surely manifest in your life.

Activity 17

All accounts positive

Want to get out of debt or have more money than you do right now? Every time you get a credit card bill, other bill, or a statement of any kind, make a copy of it and on that copy, go to the balance owed and white it out.

Next, fill in the amount of money you would like to see there instead. Say to yourself, "I am a money magnet. I have more money than I need. Every time I open a statement, it shows a positive balance." How fun!

Look at these revised statements often and spend a few moments experiencing how good it feels to have all that money in your life, how secure you feel, how free, how abundant, how responsible you are, and how generous you now can be.

By doing so, it will be so!

Activity 18

Give your cells a pep talk!

This is another activity for improving your health. I absolutely love this visualization and doing it daily for 4 months helped me to lose about 20 pounds without any special diet or exercise program. If you've seen the film What the Bleep Do We Know! you know that thoughts can literally change our very cells, affecting how well they are able to absorb nutrients, defend themselves against invaders, and metabolize.

Every day, spend 5 to 10 minutes visualizing yourself talking to your cells. If you wish to lose weight, imagine you are talking to your Weight Loss cells. If you wish to rid yourself of an illness, imagine you are talking to your Defense Against Disease cells. In your mind's eye, see these cells as characters with personalities. Imagine what they look like and how they behave.

Perhaps your Weight Loss cells are sluggish, frumpy, and suffering from poor self-esteem. Maybe they are cowering in the corners in their muumuus, afraid of you because you haven't been very nice to them in the past. Maybe your Defense Against Disease cells are like a poorly armed army in tattered uniforms, or perhaps like a disorganized football team. Use whatever images that work for you to make this visualization real.

Once you have a very clear picture of which cells you wish to talk to, what they look like, and what state they are in, you can then begin speaking to them in your imagination.

Close your eyes and start by gathering them up and sitting them down before you. If they are timid you must speak to them gently and apologize to them for past wrongs. You must win their trust back. If they are experiencing exhaustion or low morale, you must gain their confidence. Your job is to lift your cells' spirits and to get them totally revved up and excited!

Next you'll need to give them the game plan. Tell them exactly what you need them to do for you, and by when. Pass out whatever supplies they need. Assure them you believe in them and cheer them on!

If you do this every day, I promise you that health "miracles" will soon begin to occur. It worked for me with weight loss. I simply asked my cells to rev up their metabolism to maximum levels and to become lean, limber, fat fighting Charlie's Angels-type super babes! I envisioned leading them through aerobics and kickboxing exercises, seeing them getting thinner and healthier by the day. Then, I gave them instructions that they were to get me to my goal weight by a certain date. Once they got me there, I put them in maintenance mode to keep me there.

This may border on preposterous, but never underestimate the power of being preposterous! How badly do you want to change your health?

Feeling good + visualization = fulfillment of any goal.

Activity 19

The healing waterfall

This is another visualization activity for improving your health or for putting yourself in a state of feeling good. You will need to do this activity when you have the time and space to relax and get quiet. Read through the visualization first, and then take some long deep breaths, relaxing your body, and begin the meditation.

VISUALIZATION:

Imagine yourself walking along a beautiful path. When you get to the end of the path, you discover a waterfall that is flowing with water the color of gold.

As you get closer, you realize that it is not water at all, but a stream of warm, healing golden light pouring down. You walk nearer to it and see that there are stepping stones that allow you to walk right under this cascading fall of light. Imagine yourself stepping into this waterfall. Feel how warm and relaxing it is.

Now, notice that as you stand under the waterfall, feeling all of this wonderful warm light on your skin, that the light is actually penetrating through your skin and washing through the inside of your body. Feel it flowing in through the top of your head and down through every limb.

As it does so, it is washing away any disease, stress, excess fat cells, negativity, anger, fear, sadness, or other dis-ease from within you. You are getting a full physical, mental, and emotional cleansing. See all that sickness, whatever sickness you desire to rid yourself of, flowing out from your feet in dirty pools. See this dirt draining away from you and being purified as it washes away down a stream of golden light.

Stay as long as you wish. When you are ready, walk out from under the fall, feeling totally relaxed, energized, and cleansed. Step back across the stones and return along the path you came from.

Do this meditative visualization once a day for as long as you need. The results will not be immediate in physical form, but once they begin to manifest, your healing will be more effortless and speedier than before.

Activity 20

Exciting career opportunity!

This activity allows you to get clear on, and excited about achieving, your career goals. It has 2 parts:

- Do some brainstorming on what your ideal job or career looks like to you, in detail.
- Once you have a clear picture, you will then imagine yourself coming across an ad that is offering exactly the job/career opportunity you are looking for.

STEP 1: BRAINSTORM

Take out a piece of paper and answer the following questions. There is also space in the activity journal at the end of this book. If you don't have the answer to one of them, that's okay. Just answer as many as you can. Also, you may think of many answers that go beyond the questions. Please, write them down! These questions are just to get you started.

- What kind of job would you rather be doing than what you are doing now?
- If you already have the job you desire, what do you want in terms of growth, expansion, or improvement?
- What city do you want to work in?
- Do you want to go to a building each day, some days, or work only from home?
- Do you wish to travel a lot in your career? If so, to where? How often?
- What kind of physical space do you want to be in? Do you want an office of your own? Describe it in detail.
- Do you want to have a business partner(s), a boss, coworkers, any employees under you?
- Describe your ideal partner, boss, colleagues, employees – each in detail in terms of personality, skill, education level, etc.
- Who is your ideal client or customer? How many do you want?
- What amount of annual salary do you wish to have, and will some or all of this income be passive? How often do you wish to be paid? Do you want commissions, bonuses, or royalties?
- What kind of stock options, health insurance, or other benefits do you wish to have?
- How many hours a week do you wish to work? How many months of the year?

STEP 2: OPPORTUNITY FOUND

Now that you have some clarity on your new ideal career, I want you to imagine yourself surfing the internet or looking in the newspaper employment section. Suddenly, you come across a posting that describes your exact dream job or career opportunity! Not only that, when you look at the list of qualifications, it is like reading your own resume! You see that you meet or exceed every single one of the requirements.

Okay, take out another sheet of paper or use your journal space and write down that job ad. You might start with:

POSITION OPEN FOR _____ WITH _____ COMPANY

or maybe

EXCITING BUSINESS OPPORTUNITY: PARTNER WANTED!

Just keep writing, and use the brainstorm notes along with what you imagined to help you describe the job that is available. Don't worry about getting it perfect, you can edit it later! Just write!

When you are finished writing, I suggest you type up the ad and get it to look as real as it can for you. Mentally see (and emotionally feel) yourself applying for it and getting it! Take yourself on a fantasy of what it would be like to actually GET this job! It's yours! What is your new career like for you? How does it change your life? How do you now feel waking up in the morning?

Feels pretty darned good, right?

Activity 21

A perfect match

Want to attract that perfect someone into your life? All you need to do is get very, very clear on exactly who you desire and then hold onto the feelings of what having that person in your life would mean for you.

You don't want Mr. or Mrs. Right only on the surface. You must focus on the qualities and characteristics of that person. Aside from age, height and hair color, what values do you want this person to have? What kind of personality? How do you want this person to behave in a relationship? What kind of goals and aspirations would you like this person to have? What do imagine doing with this person? In what ways would your day-to-day life be different? How would it feel to have this person near you?

It is also important that you, deep in your heart, know that you are worthy of the person you desire. Like in many other areas in life, so many people short change themselves and settle for a so-so relationship, believing that settling is the closest they can get to joy, rapture and fulfillment. You deserve joy, rapture and fulfillment!

The key is to KNOW that you are perfect. You are someone's perfect mate. You are exactly what someone out there desires. We've all heard that in order to love another you must start by loving yourself. And this is very true. So let's get started.

You are going to write 2 personal ads today. One will be your ad that describes exactly what kind of mate you are seeking. The second will be an ad from your mate, in which your mate describes exactly what he or she is seeking – and that is a description of YOU!

If you have little familiarity with personal ads, it may be helpful to look at some of the websites, such as eHarmony.com or Match.com. The categories contained in several of these sites can give you lots of ideas for what to include in your own description. Remember, a good physical description is a start, but please, don't stop there!

Take some time and really think about who it is you desire to share your life with. Jot down whatever comes to mind. Then, when you are ready, make a personal ad. Here are some guidelines to get you started, but personalize this as you need it to be:

- Physical description
- Personality qualities
- Hobbies and interests
- Goals and aspirations

- Career, financial status
- Education level
- Ideal place to live
- Desires regarding children
- Values and beliefs: money, health, family, work, lifestyle, etc.
- Definition of an ideal partnership
- Life mission, purpose, and/or philosophy

Once you have finished writing your ad for your perfect mate, use the same categories to write his or her ad for a perfect mate. In every description, describe YOU. That's right. By doing this second ad you are further strengthening your request to the universe that your perfect mate finds you.

Imagine you actually went to a personals website and began looking for a partner there. You come upon the man or woman of your dreams, and then lo and behold! What they say they are looking for in a mate is a perfect description of you! Now that's a match!

Chapter 4

Feeling groovy, feeling grateful

Life has planted within us a reliable gauge for measuring our proximity to our true selves: when we get too far away, we feel rotten.

– Victoria Moran

When you're in a state of awe, you're in a persistent state of gratitude . . . . This state is the secret to fulfilling your own individual intentions, and without it, all of your most sincere efforts will amount to naught.

– Dr. Wayne Dyer

Activity 22

The gratitude journal

This is one of the simplest and most effective ways to manifest your desires. Once you've ask for what you want, you must keep yourself free of the negative feelings of lack and ingratitude. You do so by being grateful for all that you already have, not only for all that is coming to you.

Every day when you wake up, say thank you for another day. Get a notebook or a journal that is pleasing to you and take just a few moments when you wake up to write down a few things that you are grateful for. Then, before you go to bed, spend a bit more time than you did in the morning, and make a list of all the things that happened to you today that you are grateful for.

We are so used to focusing on what is wrong with or missing in our lives, that you may find yourself unable to come up with a single thing when you first start this practice. Oprah Winfrey once said during a workshop I attended, "Start with your breath!" and that was an "aha" moment for me. Start by being grateful that you are here! Keep going. Be grateful that you have clothes, food, and a roof over your head. Be grateful for your cat, for your friends, for the job that puts money in your pocket.

Even if all of the things in your life are not exactly as you would like them to be, still be grateful for them! Know this: more is on the way because of the gratitude you are now showing and feeling right now. The universe loves to be thanked, and it will respond to your thanks by giving even more.

Activity 23

Pay it forward

Did you ever see the film Pay It Forward? If you haven't I highly recommend it! This film shows the power of positive intentions, and of positive attention to other beings. Moreover, it perfectly demonstrates the Law of Circulation. What goes around comes around. If you want more love in your life, you have to be loving to others. If you want more friends, you have to be friendly to others. If you want more money, you have to give away money. On and on it goes.

I personally feel that no other activity in this book will make you feel as wonderful as this one. I have become addicted to it! All you have to do is do something nice for someone else. The only catch is this: you must do it anonymously, as often as is possible. Slip a thank you note in a coworker's box. Drop off a little treat at a neighbor's door.

It's easy for us to think of sharing a little from our savings bank of emotions, but when it comes to cash, we may find it a bit harder to let it go. Remember the Law of Circulation. Whatever you wish to get in your life, you must give away. This includes wealth. Offer to pay the toll or the parking fee of the person in the car behind you. Being in Seattle, one of my absolute favorites is to pay for the coffee drink of the next person that ends up at the front of the line at the moment I'm walking out the door.

Even if you are tight on cash (especially if this is so!) you can do something small. I started off doing this activity when I was actually in quite a bit of debt. Happily, and I believe largely because I changed my views about wealth by doing activities like this, the idea of debt is a foreign concept to me now. So go ahead and put a quarter in someone's empty parking meter – whatever you give away gets back to you!

Activity 24

I spy with my little eye . . . something wonderful!

I don't know if you ever played this game as a child. I did, and I loved it! I played it with my best friend. I would look around my environment, wherever we were, and find something that was blue, or something that was round, or something that was made of glass. My friend then had to look around and try to find the object I had chosen based on my one word description.

I discovered that this game is even more fun to play as an adult. It is so vitally important that we feel good on a daily basis and that we always keep our emotions as close to bliss as we can. Bliss is what the universe understands. Feeling good keeps us in tune to that universal energy, and it is that energy that is the channel by which all we have asked for comes to us.

So play this game every day. Play it while you are driving, or waiting in line, or sitting bored to death in a business meeting. Say to yourself the phrase **I spy with my little eye . . . something wonderful!** And then see how many wonderful things you can find.

It might be the color on a tree or on a coworker's sweater. It might be someone's smile or a car speeding by. It can be anything, so long as you find it pleasurable to notice. Even in the ugliest of environments, I guarantee there is something wonderful to gaze upon.

We are so conditioned to look only for the ugly, for the bad, for what we don't find wonderful. You must undo this conditioning, because what you choose to focus on is what your life becomes. If you only focus on negativity, ugliness, lack and problems, your daily life is filled with negativity, ugliness, lack and problems! And you will never get anything else until you begin to focus on and choose something else.

Focusing on beauty, wonder, and abundance on a daily basis not only makes you feel fabulous, it will also give you a life that is beautiful, wonderful, and abundant.

Activity 25

Goodie groceries

So many people see the glass as being half-empty rather than half-full. Even worse, some people see just an empty glass! In order to get you out of this energy draining little habit, you are going to fill up not a glass, but a goodie bag.

Imagine this life like a giant supermarket, full of such variety, offering everything imaginable, and having well-stocked shelves. The idea of shopping has associations with abundance, and so in this activity you are going to provide yourself with a visual symbol of all the abundance that exists in your life right now.

You will need a grocery or department store bag, preferably a paper one that can sit upright on its own. You will also need some scraps of paper to write on.

Here is your assignment:

Every day you are to go on a virtual mini shopping trip, selecting at least 5 items, no less. You can select more if you feel like it, but you must have at least 5 items. You will be putting these items into your goodie bag on a daily basis, watching it fill up as you proceed.

To fill your bag, simply write on a scrap of paper one 'goodie' that exists in your life, something you are grateful for. This can be something you already have, or something that you have begun intending to have in your recent visualization work. In addition to writing the item on a piece of paper, you may also drop in photos, magazine cutouts, or other visual representations of the item.

When you have selected the item, put it in your goodie bag and say, "How rich I am, how full my life is becoming!" Or something similar that works for you. Remember, the minimum is 5 goodies per day.

Do this daily until your bag becomes full. When that happens, pour out the contents and read through every single item. Talk about a shopper's high! You'll be buzzing with feelings of abundance and gratitude, sending out a beacon to the universe to bring you even more of the same! You can even go to your bag on low energy days and pour through its contents as a pick-me-up.

When your bag is full and you have gone through every item in it, I recommend putting them back in the bag and then starting a second bag to stand next to the first!

Chapter 5

Opportunity's knocking: answer the door!

When you have inspired thought, you have to trust it, and you have to act on it.
– Jack Canfield

You are never given a wish without also being given the power to make it true.

You may have to work for it, however.

– Richard Bach

Activity 26

Express delivery!

Express Delivery! is an outstanding way to improve your intuition, leaving you more open to creative solutions, insights and action steps when they present themselves as part of the Answering to your Asking.

Whenever you are stuck for an answer to an issue you are working on, or even if you are just waiting in line or commuting somewhere and want to use that time to work on your manifestations, imagine in your mind's eye a courier from your Universal Delivery Service appearing next to you and saying "Express Delivery!"

In your imagination, the messenger hands you an envelope and disappears again. You open the envelope and inside it is a single sheet of paper that contains a short message. You pull out the paper and read whatever the message says.

This message will be exactly what you need to hear. It may be an idea, an affirmation, just a single word, or the name of someone. Know that because the universe is abundant and good, it is impossible to ever receive a negative message. Even if the page is blank, that is a message that you need to put more focus on listening to messages! So don't be apprehensive that you will receive a bad omen or hostile message – it simply isn't possible.

Even if the message doesn't make sense at first, keep thinking about its significance. Ask yourself:: What does this mean to me? Why did I attract this message into my life at this moment? How does this message help me solve the problem I have right now?

You'll get better at it with practice, and pretty soon the Universal Delivery Service will send you messages every day. Your intuition will become so strong that you'll be able to interpret these messages instantly, with no effort, and make real positive changes in your life.

Activity 27

Signs (the billboard game)

This is another activity for reconnecting to your intuitive powers. As you begin your day, ask that the universe send you an important sign, something that is exactly what you need for today. Then, as you go about your day, pay attention to billboards, ads, or other "messages" out there.

At some point in the day, one of those signs will just jump out at you. It may be the entire message on the sign, or it might be only one word that strikes you. When this happens, take a few moments to reflect on the meaning of this message and then say thank you to the universe for delivering it to you.

I practice this on a daily basis and have been doing so long enough that I now get powerful messages. It was through a sign on the side of a bus that I got the message to write this book!

Activity 28

I must be dreaming

Do you want to know once and for all what is happening when you dream at night? Here's what dreams are: they are status checks on where you are at in the process of attracting what you desire. Your higher consciousness uses metaphors because it can't communicate in words – it doesn't think or reason. It's up to you to decipher its messages and interpret them.

There are tons of dream interpretation books out there, and every one of them is totally useless to you. Why? Because your dreams are 100% unique to your own situation. By understanding what your dreams are saying, you can see what your thoughts are attracting and either be confirmed that you are on the right track, or realize that you need to change direction. It's so much easier to change something before it shows up than it is after it has already manifested!

2 things to keep in mind:

- People in your dream aren't about the real people in your life; rather, they are merely there as a metaphor. So don't panic if you kiss your boss in a dream! Maybe it really means that you are about to welcome a new career into your life.
- A nightmare doesn't mean something bad is about to happen. Rather, it is more likely that you haven't been paying attention to more subtle messages from your intuition and so your higher consciousness is trying to get you to listen up!

Instead of worrying whether you're really going to be run over by a bus, try and decide what the bus represents. Is there an opportunity to get from where you are to where you want to be (the bus) staring you right in the face, but you haven't noticed it?

The only way to get better at interpreting the messages from your higher consciousness is to practice, practice, practice. I personally think that the best way to do this is to keep a dream log, or a dream journal. Each night before you go to sleep, place your journal and a pen on your nightstand and say to yourself, "I intend to remember my dreams upon waking."

When you do wake, take a few moments to recall any dreams and then write them down. You don't have to write a novel, just note some key words and phrases, enough that when you return to your notes later you'll be able to recall the dream's highlights. Leave enough space for coming back and making interpretational notes later.

To interpret your dream, ask yourself these questions:

- What is this dream a metaphor for?
- What does such-and-such person represent?
- What does this dream say regarding what I'm about to attract into my physical reality?

Write down your answers. This might be hard at first, but just like parallel parking, you can only get better at it by practicing.

Activity 29

Clutterclearing

One of the most effective activities you can do is to make space in your life for what is to come. Physical clutter is a mirror of the mental and emotional clutter within you. Often, when we are overly focused on the past instead of on our future, it will show up as clutter in our lives.

When your space is full there is no room for new treasure to enter. When your mind and heart are hanging on to what was, there is no room for your dreams to manifest! What are you hanging on to that needs to be let go?

Is your closet full of clothing that no longer fits? Are your cupboards full of items you no longer use? Do you have pieces in your home that you don't even like that much because you feel guilty about letting them go? Are you a "someday I might need this?" kind of person? You must let all of these things go so that the energy of both your physical and emotional space is uncluttered, clear, restful, organized, and ready for all of your desires to come.

Clutterclearning is NOT the same thing as organizing. I'm not talking about stacking that pile of old magazines into neat piles in a fancy holding case – I'm talking about getting that pile out of your house if it is not serving your current purpose!

There are only 2 rules to follow when deciding what to keep and what to clear out:

RULE 1

The item must serve A) a functional purpose B) an aesthetic purpose C) both. If it doesn't have a functional and/or an aesthetic purpose for you – RIGHT NOW AT THIS TIME IN YOUR LIFE – then it must go!

RULE 2

If you don't LOVE IT, you must let it go!

I recommend that you not try to clutterclear your entire house in a day. This can be an exhilarating, but also exhausting, process. Start with one area only. Take your time.

Only do this activity when you are in a strong, energetic mood. If you are feeling drained, nostalgic, or emotionally vulnerable, this is not a good time to do this activity.

If you do this when you are feeling energetic and ready to make changes in your life, go for it! You will feel fabulous at the end of this exercise!

To do this effectively, I recommend you make 3 piles:

- KEEP PILE – you use this item now and you really like it
- TOSS/DONATE PILE – you never or rarely use this item and/or you don't like this item
- COME BACK TO PILE – you don't use this item, but you feel an emotional attachment to this item and you're not ready to part with it yet.

Options for handling your COME BACK TO pile:

1. Remake it: Can you remake this item into something else that you will use? For example, I was helping a friend do this when we came to her wedding dress. She knew she would never wear her wedding dress again, but she couldn't part with it. So instead, I suggested she turn the material into throw pillows for her bed. That way, every time she touches those pillows, she'll remember her wedding day.
2. Gift it: Do you have a close friend or a relative you could give the item to? That way, you still get to see the item and also know that you have given a gift to someone who truly appreciates it.
3. Return to it: Come back to this pile again 1 week later and see if you are ready to part with it now that you've had a little emotional distance. If you STILL can't part with it, find a way to USE it in your home! Display it or use it, but don't let it sit in a box.

Tip:

Have a trusted friend help you out with this project. They can be excellent coaches for keeping you on track when you hit an emotional bump in the road and want to keep everything.

Activity 30

Nothing doing

This is the last, and the most crucial, activity in this entire book. Do not be fooled by its simplicity: You are to do nothing for 10 to 15 minutes every single day. That's right, absolutely nothing. It is in this time of doing nothing that you are allowing all you've asked for to manifest. The purpose of this activity is to quiet your ego self, to get it out of the way so that your higher self can do its work. In quiet, you connect to spirit.

You can call it meditation, cat napping, or spacing out, but do nothing! Clear your mind of all thoughts. Take several deep breaths and allow yourself to just relax and BE. If you have a hard time emptying your mind, as most people do, try repeating this little mantra to yourself over and over:

I put my higher self in the driver's seat. It knows where we are going. There is nothing I need to do now but sit back and enjoy the ride.

About the author

MELODY LARSON IS an accomplished teacher, life coach, writer, and consultant. From her early career as an instructor to subsequent careers in instructional design, staff and faculty training, and organizational development, she has always sought to inspire personal growth and transformation in others.

Recognizing this "desire to inspire" as the passionate thread weaving in and out of her professional work, Melody began applying her skills to the design of personal development seminars, workshops, and coaching sessions. For more than 10 years, she has been helping others to uncover their life purpose and to transform their goals and dreams into reality.

An avid student herself, her current quest is to learn to inspire others to expand not only at the human level, but at the spiritual level as well. Recognizing that a consciousness-raising is taking place globally, it is her intention to join the ranks of those teachers dedicated to casting a light into the world regarding the limitless, eternal, co-creative beings that we all are.

Melody currently lives in the Seattle area. She welcomes comments about your experiences with this book and can be emailed at: melody@abundanceforbeginners.com.

My activity journal

Activity 1: Getting out of Shouldville

Activity 3: Bliss list blitz

Activity 4: Your perfect day

Activity 6: Prison break

Activity 7: Body talk

Activity 8: Pamper your senses

Activity 10: Intention statements

Activity 11: What/Why wheels

Activity 13: Grant letters

Activity 18: Give your cells a pep talk!

Activity 20: Exciting career opportunity!

Activity 21: A perfect match

Activity 22: The gratitude journal

Activity 28: I must be dreaming

.ates

9 781425 752576